Partial
Genius

Partial Genius

prose poems

MARY BIDDINGER

Black
Lawrence
Press

www.blacklawrence.com

Executive Editor: Diane Goettel
Cover & Book Design: Amy Freels

Published 2019 by Black Lawrence Press.
Printed in the United States.

For the French club presidents: past, present, and future.

CONTENTS

HISTORICAL ACHIEVEMENTS

Very few lives of the presidents mirrored lives of the saints, but there are exceptions. Certain children fall into step after anything titled "a challenge." The rest of us sneak out the back door and watch it close behind us. Generally speaking, the presidents conformed in choice of garments and complied with rules such as what to burn and what not to kill, which was most things.

I found myself at a bar asking anyone who would listen about whether today's children still play with paper dolls, and surprisingly this was taken as a brash come-on by the men and women surrounding the only pinball machine that still functioned. I would have demonstrated how I used to balance my smoke while on the commode but then remembered the paper dolls and didn't.

Waiting in the vestibule of urgent care sent me back to a show about a country veterinarian where once somebody found an unidentifiable animal and attempted to let it name itself, and then to direct the nurse how best to feed it, and eventually they realized it wasn't alive after all, much like the results passed to me in waxed paper, except I was thrilled and strutted out like an elk.

In the future all my friends would be painting the same fake sunflower and calling it art, while I continued waving from atop my pile of deconstructed charcoal kestrels. Someday the right old rich man would find me, and the street value of my juvenilia would skyrocket, while the wrong old rich man told jokes about lives of the presidents from a damp bar stool of complete ignorance.

I watched a film where the highway was the protagonist and was supposed to garner our pity, but I was so jealous I took off two of my three shirts and stood up before the credits. One year I wrote "mouth" across my knuckles for Halloween and exited the pep rally before the microphone was switched on, flocks of balloons still humping the plastic bags designated to contain them.

THE JOLLY ANCHOR

It was no place for a girl. You couldn't use your words. Somebody exhaled a story involving a shipwreck and a sandwich, no idea which came first, and certainly not the woman wearing a fetishist's latest metallurgy. We were all waiting for "the crisis" to arrive. Sweating on it. Trying to catch it in our lungs. Making it into a fish, then netting it. Or maybe that was me. And maybe the captain was you.

Everything short of writing me a vocabulary list, tying a blindfold, walking around the room with a lit match, a game of *identify the song I'm humming incorrectly*, too small to be a lemon but too big for a lime, quick allusion to turn of the century (the sexy one), pathos regarding bookish tendencies or a history in dirty little towns, rudeness to the wait staff, a stolen soup spoon, naked beneath greasy overcoat.

Do not omit certain grandiose statements. Not delusions of grandeur; those are implicit. Where to begin? With "I am Jesus and you are my sister and my wife." With intercepted calls that supposedly ended up on your rotary phone, as if by divine providence. If I could say one thing to the President it would be that you are a terrible girl and need punishing quick before you change back into a lake I forgot you said.

Take two somewhat gorgeous strangers and put them in a gorge. Conjoin two lethargic wasters and sit them at the bar. Place one bear on the ridge and the other on her back with a fish. Give her a fix. You kept talking about when the boat would come to take you away, and at first I thought it was a song, and gave you credit for proficiency in Americana, but that, like everything else, was an artifact of a fraudulent bygone time.

Imagine being hospitalized on a boat. The infirmary the size of someone's back. All you could hold was ropes and your own knees. Someone giving both of us tattoos. Things can be surprising and sore, but what matters is who is in control of the ship's wheel, and who is bailing down below. Who dashes the brains of the violin on her way out the door. Who is left like a blood stain on a bale of burning straw.

SKILL GAMES

My earliest memory was a costumed prospector biting into a bullet of golden chocolate. By then I was already too large for the ornamental railroad, but that didn't stop my father from folding all my folds into the front seat, then waving as the engine croaked forward. I wasn't a baby's baby. At christening I gripped chain crosses that relatives slathered around my neck. My mother refused the heirloom ankle bracelet, claiming it looked like bondage, but I don't think she meant it that way.

Decades later I would garner recognition for my scholarly article on the withdrawal method. It involved substantial field research and observable outcomes. I pasted Venn diagrams on the walls of my carrel in the library. Thankfully the philosophy professor who shared that space never tampered with my wet mounts. I had to relate everything to back to post-structuralism. My prospectus earned a special commendation from the graduate college.

Sometimes I have a dream of walking onto the stage of an amphitheater, thronged by fans of my intellectual property. And then I realize it's just another job interview. No matter how many times I do it, and how much the jitters fade and the adrenaline kicks in, whatever the operating system, hooking up projection cables will give me palpitations. I pretend to be in my previous incarnation as figure model for the rehabilitative art class, where I was just a series of widening circles.

I didn't expect infiltration of the natural family planning seminar to be so depressing. Sure, I made great casseroles, but they were for somebody else's husband. I stuttered and told everyone my name was Madrigal. Like the feast. We started with a familiar prayer. Halfway through I shimmied out the rectory window and landed in a boudoir of wet, trembling yews. Maybe I shouldn't have mentioned that it was all old news to me, or quoted my substantive findings.

Of course there were one or more men who made up the control group. Afterwards we'd ride the train together, intentionally choosing the un-flocked seats. There was a downtown apartment building where children packed the rooftop pool at all hours. I'd cross and un-cross my legs according to what emanated from my headphones. Maybe I would also sing a little, then phone in an order for spicy take-out. Next door to the restaurant, ninety watts of blue neon shouted: skill games.

APOLOGY TOUR

Maybe I'm a little rusty in the saddle. Maybe I'm the little rust stain on a pair of white pants. A customer always has a right to be right. I was not the ideal girl for a spinning basket or giant sugar cone. My background was not in wastepaper management.

Let's listen to Black Sabbath and inhale the rage of vinyl car seats. Please forget how I stormed the bank in my sugar-colored nightie, trying to cash in. Remember me the way I was at the bonnet festival: perfect dimensions for filling anything bound with ribbon.

If somebody offers to buy you a drink called All My Promises Are Bullshit, recall the time you got in a scuffle with the bus driver over cotton candy. Today teenagers drink cotton candy vodka and wear clear, potent undergarments. You don't need to know how I know this.

At my high school reunion, everyone wore the same t-shirt: *Same Crap, Different Century.* I think they meant *decade*, but 1992 was not a year of precision. Even the virgins were divorced at least once. I provided my concise biography in two words: near miss.

In the university that I shall invent after becoming rich, every class will be as classless as the last. Perhaps occasionally I will offer a seminar. Education is the last luxury you said before peeling off your shirt and captaining a boat to the edge of the world.

Describe your genius in thirty words or less. Eat the best page of your favorite book. Go camping but with no water or twine. Make your skirts into a sort of tent. Bless those who curse you. Slap your freedom down then let it ride.

SACRÉ-CŒUR

Back when I was getting high I kept losing my gloves—not one, but both of them, every time. So much for the theory of a mysterious other in your duplicate bedroom hoarding all the lost gloves, and the hope of some day getting married next to a rain barrel and some grackles.

When the social worker asked about how my life had been effected (sic) I mentioned that all food tasted like Windex and sometimes the sound of clocks was a powerful aphrodesiac (sic). I went to class and then purchased large scoops of cherry ice cream, but only to watch them melt.

The only subject that resonated was French. I found some dough and gave my skit about the Bois de Boulogne extra verisimilitude, which meant a man with a weapon, the wrong phone number, a red scarf (not too tight!), and a door that wouldn't yield to the sound of muffled accordion.

I decided I would sit in the library and sneeze until somebody stopped me. I decided I would lurk the quad and contemplate the big questions. The funny thing is that I did way better at mandatory brunches. I didn't wear sweaters. I was not intimidated by lengthy menus.

I managed to desecrate a number of unholy texts, but in a holy way that demonstrated "an advanced sense of presence... determined to no longer use sex... self-diagnosed genius... internalized feelings of superiority." Everyone gave me legal pads for my birthday.

Legend states that if you kiss the marble steps at 4 am during your first week, you'll stay in school forever. Alternately, it states that you may consider this previous gift to be much like living inside a whale. When you find your whale, it will be packed with gloves.

SOME TRUTHS

All the other women had husbands. Instead I talked about my collection of pig masks. It was clear I was a city girl. You just had to look at my fingernails and the corners of my mouth, which were both square. Clearly I didn't get the dipstick joke. Maybe that joke was on me, like a wet sweater, a therapeutic leach.

Once I had a job serving lunch to old folks. The application process involved whistling and arranging wooden spoons in order from largest to largest. Mostly I sliced bananas into coins and dehydrated them, picked up the green phone and breathed when callers asked what my name was, what was for dinner.

My roommate signed us up for a puppetry workshop. Anxiety attacks began about ten days before the first class. All those Styrofoam balls without galaxies. Suddenly I was topless again, attempting to bend over and fetch a stray balloon string. Who has a birthday party on a balcony in mid-January?

I loved being around smart people when they were neither pontificating nor mansplaining. Except if they were discussing Nietzsche as if he was William James, the entire world a conspiracy tapping holes in pint glasses and hollow legs, like my beauty was something constructed by a god and not two bored teenagers.

When I walked into the hallowed basement of the courthouse, I felt like a manifesto or a particularly bold haircut. Perhaps it was the absence of religion, or the compressed dimensions of the bathroom stalls, where nobody could have ever worked out a way to fuck, regardless of previous circus employment.

The best part of figure skating was getting cut. Not by an errant skate, but by the cruel rim of sequins on every elastic opening. Even now, if somebody utters the word *footloose* I'm a bodice of thorns. My back covered with shimmery polyester bologna. Something stirring the confines of my braided hair.

TROUBLE SHIRT

Mailing heaps of paper isn't unusual, but when the pants started arriving in my office mail slot (postage due) I couldn't blink them away. I swear one crumpled set of brown corduroys was still warm from your knees, or maybe it was hot in the van that day. I've forgotten most of what might be deemed tender, because I wasn't looking for it. Nobody cares if you're loved when it's just a little.

Various past mistakes wanted to make amends. Yet I was no longer the girl with a hammer in her hand, teetering in front of a stained glass depiction of the Last Supper. Restaurants that had housed our fondest memories were boarded up. In the old days that never would have stopped us, but now I had a mortgage and you had your various failed campaigns, including me.

It was just like a shell game, but with hands. And maybe I shouldn't be saying this, but it lasted a lot longer than expected. Suddenly we had to imagine what the future fashions would be, to avoid wearing them on accident. Such as really boisterous scarves, an oversized watch that you hitched tight around my ankle, then some reference to Faulkner and a whole lot of exhaling followed by distant interjections from the bell tower.

When I said I wanted arugula for my birthday, I wasn't being whimsical. A man can trouble you all year, a bee in the bedsheets, a bucket of paint in your mushroom soup. And to say that you were my ally was at times a specious claim. Wars have been waged over less than clandestine attendance at a funeral with a woman described as *a pile of outdated bylaws*.

Perhaps you should know that I still have my trouble shirt. In our messages about past outfits, we have been careful to avoid it. Let's go back to the day that we tried to find the magnetic springs. Instead we lost the wheel of the truck and talked about the plastic music box you loved as a child. And how then I danced like a coil of ribbon wrapped around a tree.

BASTILLE DAY

So much light is just litter. Stray goblets tossed in trenches, torn undergarments decorating the most slack lawn ornaments. And let's get one thing straight: you were not the figurehead on my ship until you jumped overboard. Of course, when you jumped overboard it was into me.

Some might demand: where is your pride, little birthday figurine? There's a new you for every year, and the previous version gets pushed to the back of the rack, next to the freeze-dried starfish. One time you tried to figure out the equation that began: how much salt? We know how that ended up.

Something about black lace, except it was actually pen marks, and blue. It was the way to disaster an arcade. Often the best prizes are beyond reach of the metal arm. But that didn't keep me from telling you a ghost story under a damp, transparent bed sheet.

The first night you saw me you mentioned how badly I needed to be stormed. I thought you were drawing upon your rich continental heritage, established 1789 or thereabouts. Blown out beggars on the street didn't bother asking for change. We sent your sandwich back twice.

Weren't we all damp, transparent bed sheets back then? Some crafty mother would knot us and dip our clots into natural dyes. Maybe a shy finch would let loose a flurry across our tender edges. Mostly, we spread ourselves out and waited for it.

EMPTY LOCKET SYNDROME

Everything is easy when you don't try. Locating the greenest liquor in a store. Looking natural in a cowboy hat encrusted with rhinestones usually reserved for failed showgirls. One time my man drove me under the overpass and we stumbled through a tent city. The greenest liquor under the overpass was inadequate.

All the homemaking magazines recommended drafting a list of pros and cons. I attempted tarts from scratch, but they looked more like vermin than a vacation for the tongue. Since when did we need to think of putting our bodies on loan? I was more than ready to surrender. His apartment was not air conditioned. The furniture was borderline historic.

I was not one to judge, but naked on a couch that was mostly wood, with a few cushions bearing pioneer-inspired prints, I thought I felt reverberations of a chainsaw. We read aloud from a short story and over-brewed the coffee. Ventured out early and had to make our own sun hats from newspaper. Several times we stopped so I could pin his boot back together.

For a couple of people who didn't care about appearances, we certainly appeared. He'd shove a slip of paper into my pocket: *Do we look pretentious?* It was just an abandoned bus stop where sometimes pensioners holed up with bottles and unfortunate songs. He told me about a painter who developed a fatal habit of drinking his lover's perfume.

I prayed at the wrong church. Loved the cafeteria for its potent cleaners. At home he kept several inches of water in the tub, for emergency. Someday we would all thank him, as we wiped our lips dry. The same song played back to back on the jukebox. In a photo booth, we took pictures of ourselves ripping up all of our previous pictures.

THE SUBJECT POOL

Somebody had to stand outside the men's room. I was aware of other places. There were about twenty years where I could consider myself not a statistic, but a determined trout attempting to make good in a reasonably uncontaminated stream. And then, the whoosh of nuclear fallout. To think that at one point people used this water for medicinal purposes. Now it's coveted by vengeful ex-lovers.

In high school, runaway horses would try to scare us on our walk home. It took way more than a wayward fetlock to frighten me. We'd pool money and split an éclair from the bakery. Walk down Eastman with extra purpose. And then all that awful hoof clatter. One of the horses was still wearing a show saddle, but it was flipped upside down. I tried to stop him and take it off, but he cantered away.

Have you ever made love to someone who insisted on calling it *making love*? And why didn't you stop then? Because he stood below your bedroom window for a long time. He knew more than you did, and not about small engine repair or animal glands. He would call you from a payphone and you'd unfurl your outdated city map and go seek his intersection in an air conditioned taxi.

None of the story problems in high school explained why I was the kind of girl no one would give a ring to. Yet I did great on the entrance exam. The psychology department pulled me out of the subject pool, paid me to view slides while wearing a headdress of sensors. I'm sorry I arrived at college statistics II wiping glue off my forehead. I yearned for a remake of the Stanford Prison Experiment.

When you hold me, please know that you are not holding me. On graduation day, I watched a man tattoo *AU COURANT* around my thigh. It was like sitting in stopped traffic, not realizing every soul on the bus was looking down into your car, watching you readjust. Ten years later, I crawled up vinyl stairs for a paycheck, spent it all on gasoline to write my name in flames on the lawn.

THE CRAFT

I was so good at being the new girl at school that after a while I pondered climbing into random academy windows and presenting myself to the headmaster. In my purse I carried flash cards and a disassembled diorama. It was a multipurpose diorama that could be customized to represent the Bastille or a 1950s suburban soda shop. The main difference was the contents of the barrels. Once I showed up at my new high school holding a red solo cup filled with coconut malt liquor.

People talk about how high school was the highlight of their existence. For me, it was like being held captive in an enormous sock drawer, with only a pack of matches for entertainment. My best friend was a Swedish purple-leaved ivy that I snuck into bed with me, and sometimes carried into the shower, because it can rain all the time. The plant also had magical properties that kept me safe from the cheerleaders.

Some girls sit around in a circle and query the planchette regarding lost classmates from the class of 1987. Others ask the devil to lift their freckles. I smuggled my Swedish purple-leaved ivy into the tarot trailer on M-20. Drove down the cruise strip blasting Alien Sex Fiend, plant buckled in the back seat. The yearbook would declare me most witchy, but that was due to my AP chemistry scores. Nobody who could actually fly would sit through a two hour exam.

I wanted to drink something out of an upside down umbrella. Traditionally this would involve a straw, but I wasn't a traditionalist. How could I accomplish such a feat without witchcraft? That's an amateur question. The gymnasium couldn't contain my desire to transform into three versions of myself, each better than the last. This was back before I understood that everything was an adventure. Previous to that, it was all a parlor game. There was a profound difference.

PARTIAL CREDIT SYNDROME

That summer I could not stop sneezing. I wasn't addicted, but will admit to loving the abs that resulted, and how easily I could skip to the front of any line. It was time to reread *Go Ask Alice* while drinking Tab cola. The trees in my yard seemed a little more vigorous than usual.

Some people have the honor of witnessing miracles. Hedgehogs weed the garden then appear in tidy aprons. Statues scrawl and re-scrawl their own obscenities. I had no idea that twenty years later I would be bobbing in a cold lake, like sea-trash, until fished out.

Of course, I did not want to be fished out. I had a stomach weighted with naan and warm champagne. All of my decisions were sound. I was the message inside the bottle, and the bottle, and the rip tide. I was heading to Wisconsin the hard way.

My diary entries were written with silver pen that had a white outline. I tried to trace my hand, but missed a finger. Thanked the lord I'd never need to stuff anything with tissues. I pulled up the bottom of my terrycloth romper, and then folded down the top.

When I claim that I had a low tolerance that summer, I am not referencing a little gin in the Fresca. All the newspapers gabbed on about a referendum, or a mother lode. Sometimes my parents had to hand-feed me slivers of cheese. The top forty stopped at thirty five.

VOIR DIRE

The first time I got robbed I walked away feeling strangely free. Back then I had less. You could still be a slayer and a scholar. I did things because they were due, not because they were right.

Somebody planted a cross in the woods. It made people feel bad about their choices, which was the point. My grandmother provided this footnote in her Jeep. She was well beneath the speed limit.

Apparently lawyers care what you wear on the stand. The only thing in my bag was a peanut butter sandwich, and a guard insisted on scanning it with a wand. They voted against my scarf.

Halfway through constructing a stone rosary I decided maybe it was time to quit praying. I wrote myself a series of one word notes. Read an article on how to clean your diamond ring at home.

The sky bitched about its cramps. We were doing awful things to it. In the rec room I watched another contamination tragedy. The machine bore a lipstick-red hood, like all criminals of the time.

I tried to look like a college student, not an abandoned runway at the shuttered municipal. When asked for identification, I remembered not to flee. I could not save every empty paper cup.

The courthouse lobby was like a shanty I'd once built of remaindered ceiling tiles. Flinty, close. I felt like the only one who hated advertisements. The jurors sang into their Cokes.

For some women it's a dilemma where to take your diamond ring for a quality scrub. A familiar counter or an anonymous booth. The moment you hand it over you belong only to yourself.

NOTRE DAME DE PARIS

What was left wasn't her, and it wasn't me, and it wasn't a visage lifted from any of the posters that decorated our shared bedroom. One day she was there, and the next she was reportedly giving hand jobs in the back booth at the Ram's Horn and then she disappeared completely.

I thought I did well filling out the application. I underlined certain passages for emphasis and to demonstrate how lively I could be and how dependable. My mother said there was no way I would get hired by a bookstore due to my imperial attitude, and she was right. But this was pie.

I heard once that a classmate offered an entire semester's worth of French instruction in the 20 minute cab ride it took to go from Roosevelt to Lawrence Avenue. Okay, that was me, but it was a noteworthy academic excursion for the discerning traveler with no surplus time on his hands.

To be honest, there were days when I ground my cheek into the grass and acknowledged that it could never get better, and it didn't. When's the last time you got to boycott two simultaneous parties and secret a soft shell crab in your pink purse? I didn't think so.

Of all the adolescents and post-adolescents and post-post-adolescents huddled in the doorway of Notre Dame de Paris, only one was wearing a pathetic high school football jersey beneath her manteau, and that was her, but only because she was emulating me.

Sometimes old friends are like a packet of corn that occupies minimal space in the back of the freezer. Other times they're a rice fire instead. She was the empty pâte brisée I ate off a brochure on the bus. I was just another an old church packed with jackets and sermons.

PROCREATION MYTH

Let's not underplay the role that alcohol has in this equation. Two blue jays fighting to the death in the courtyard, and all you can think about is flinging the Ortho Tri-Cyclen pills one by one into a catfish pond. The next day, in line behind a mother of three at the grocery checkout, you're ready to mainline a week's worth of those candies.

Everyone told you *have faith*. Just wait. Put it in the hands of god, not in the hands of ____, who is only your god, but not universally recognized. A day or two after the surgery, you meet ____ at the coffee shop (neither yours nor his) and discreetly show him your zipper of staples. It makes him want a second cup of coffee. You're that metal.

A summer job in boudoir photography sounds great until you're suffering hell cramps and the clients need extra fluffing of their boas, or extra profound eyeliner. *I hate Joan Jett*, or *Fuck Whitesnake*, the wrong lights pulsating at the wrong time, all the best props tumbling from the wall in unison, not sure if it's right to be relieved or not.

A few weeks into the poetry workshop and you let it slip. Of course, this is at the dance club where your professor and several classmates followed you after drinking Bass Ale and listening to reggae on the jukebox. Why did you carry a spare wig and sequined vest in your backpack? The same reason some people have two Chapsticks in one pocket.

It's probably too late now to mention this, but there was always a moment when I bucked my back in unison with the strobe light and felt I made my own sort of animal. My favorite movie will always be *Coal Miner's Daughter*, even if I am vomiting in a graffiti-frescoed bathroom. *Stop*, the poster declared, *the life you make may be your own*.

THE HAUNTED MINUTE

I'm pretty confident in claiming that I tell the best ghost stories. Not just the one about how a pair of bulldozers knocked down my childhood bungalow in thirty five minutes. Nor the tale of what my mother really kept in the locked jewelry box. I learned pretty early that everyone was dirty, but in different ways. Most locks were dirty, too.

Let's imagine we are stuck in an elevator together. When I was a kid, Dutch elm disease ravaged the neighborhood. That was before crack. Now every time I ride an elevator I think of the story my uncle told about the glass eye. It had a tiny witch inside the artificial pupil. That story wasn't scary. I'm not sure where he found the bloody handkerchief.

You might sneer at the idea of a haunted rope, but you won't be laughing when your car teeters at the edge of a ravine, and all you have is dental floss to secure your bumper. Sometimes during sex I whisper *Where's my golden arm?* So far only one man has caught the allusion. I turned him into a majestic sugar maple, and frequently picnic in his shadow.

One late afternoon we both looked out the window and said *oh my god*. And then we vanished like the hitchhikers that we were. We abandoned our figurative jackets in the back seat of the proverbial car. Swore each other off, and then fell off the wagon within the same night. My building was an elevator building, yours a primitive walk-up.

Are the minutes themselves haunted, or is that our fault? You might remember the apex of our love affair to be the time you had to employ olive oil to get duct tape out of my bangs. I might consider it our first trip to the broken fountain. We looked into the water and saw the reflection of our stooped, aged selves. They were complete strangers to each other.

CAUTIONARY FILM

When I was declared free of scoliosis, something lifted out of me. I wrote in my small notebook: you will enjoy a life of mostly clear diagnoses. For once, I cut through people's back yards instead of sticking to the sidewalks with the other milquetoasts. At the Walgreens, I exhibited radically poor posture and bought candy cigarettes, which never made it out of my sock drawer.

It was 1987, and if you had sex you would die of AIDS. It was extra tragic considering all the illegitimate babies you would inevitably leave behind. I tried to combat this by eating an excess of asparagus and throwing myself into the rhododendrons. My childhood dollhouse had a tiny father with a sleek, eventless crotch. Once I discovered him buried to the cheeks in a litter box.

In the cautionary film, it was always an art teacher or school photographer who took inappropriate liberties. I found liberties completely appropriate when my art teacher cold-cocked a star hockey player in the parking lot. I wrote in my small notebook: you have a gift for traveling undetected. But then I resented the invisibility, and considered purple hair.

Later I would hold a modest role in a small production that almost made it to select art houses. My character folded a pair of khakis and then cried a little. Too bad Miss Blaine would never have a chance to retract her criticisms from the high school theatrical arts clinic. My character had no name or face, but her command over the scene was irrefutable.

CONSOLATION PRIZE

I frequented a desolate pie shop. The drinks were lukewarm and all songs on the jukebox were about dying. I did not do this because I thought it would make me authentic. I was lukewarm about everything, often felt war was imminent. I lived in a neighborhood full of homeowners terrified of being first to roll the trash cans down to the curb.

Intermediate violin class taught me to just keep on going. One afternoon a fluorescent bulb exploded over first chair, and I thanked my stars for being second. Someday I wanted to be a lady who carried a small cat in a medium wooden basket. Nobody considered this a morbid wish at the time. For years, the ribbons I wore in my hair were only mildly ironic.

At the wolf sanctuary, they told me I had to play with the almost-wolves. Some of them were people in costumes who rubbed their backs against tree trunks. Later I settled down with some rhubarb and a book filled with blank pages. My friends had recommended this place as a stopgap measure, but they had never set foot on the property.

Sometimes my hair wakes me up. Other nights I bolt out of bed and start building a shack from the contents of my desk. Don't judge, but there are days when I think about digging a hole for myself, or making a sign: I am not the only one who can help you. The sign would have a conventional font, and a red border, to foster a sense of harmony.

If asked about my most glorious moment, I'll confess that dancing in a completely empty studio in delirious wee hours of Houghton, Michigan was better than any night beneath a sugar maple. I can't describe the glory of the sound system, but music will never again be such a bottomless quarry. It was the late summer of 1988. I knew absolutely nothing.

THE NEW TESTAMENT EFFECT

Years ago, all we had to worry about was the occasional holiday headache. I was vulnerable enough to purchase anything preceded by the word *ultra*. For my thirtieth birthday, I asked for a tornado, but it ended up mostly noise and swirling leaves, like any other early summer Thursday.

I am Catholic, so of course I don't know the Bible. My family did not go out for breakfast. We didn't evangelize beyond our own intrinsic appeal. My grandfather started walking home before the end of Mass. Our neighborhood felt liberated, not confined, by the presence of electric train tracks.

Somebody once promised me that soon everything would be completely different. Birds underwater, mirrors framed with breakfast cereal. There's something great about washing your feet in the kitchen sink, as long as it's not your sink. I recommend being in love with a high-end house sitter.

He might break a light bulb and not clean it up. There's a reason no one has kept him. But in early June, before knowing the things you'll later know, such as the birth dates and eye colors of your respective, separate children, it's possible to suspend disbelief. Small trees might die without watering.

Your favorite part of the Bible was that story about the flood, but it was mostly the thought of luxuriating on a ship between camels and zebras and cranes and their vast, auspicious futures. Maybe summer was the wrong season. The sidewalks so dry, and no need to bother locating the oars.

HORIZON-FREE LIVING

After a few hours in a paddock with the ram, I thought maybe it wasn't so bad. I was known for overreacting. Perhaps the fence wasn't buzzing with electricity. My clothes felt less muddy than anticipated. It was like staying at a bed and breakfast: more rustic than the brochure, shadowed by excessive history. The history was mine. The ram had not felt a human hand in years.

Every time the phone rang, I dropped what I was holding. Most of the calls were from a self-proclaimed *licensed technician*. I attempted to explain my concerns to the hold music. Somebody was asking somebody else for money on live television. A politician pushed his pamphlet through a crack under a door. I contemplated my unfinished landscape painting in the attic.

Seminars in animal husbandry are mostly about management. One teacher held up my breakout budget for everyone's scrutiny. What I wanted to say was that I had years of relevant experience. Such a statement would not fit into a single spreadsheet cell. In my early writings, I had a tendency to reverse the words *scared* and *sacred*, to the point that my man became hallowed.

I figured it wouldn't hurt to sing to the ram. At this moment the rain had turned to mist, as in a grocery store broccoli corridor. In previous dreams, I had traversed the countryside with the ram on a silver ribbon. Commissioned an appropriately scaled saddle. Watched as he approached a basket of freshly-scrubbed leeks. Held his wise face steady for the priest's blessing.

Of all the things I scrawled on my man's back window, I never reconsidered the part about flexible long term investments and reversibility. I was known for adopting my own version of the truth. He prepared his dinner, and then set it aside. I was the kind of person who could abandon a painting before the edges were completely dry. He never listened to the same song twice.

MOST BELOVED ROLES

I have always distrusted floating candles. Feared dark pillows impersonating departed cats. One evening my lover was highly intoxicated and said he was going to play the conductor like a cello. Did he mean a symphony, or the electronic voice that prohibited litter and radio playing? Choose a sphere, the public intellectual said to us, not understanding we had already committed.

When a scout propositioned me it was for rock opera and there was no talk of a merry widow. I recall the exact moment my childhood friend ceased being so, despite two decades of camaraderie, all because I had more batter in my crêpe pan. Had I been a stereotype, I would have peeled back the skin of a photo album and inserted a piece of loose leaf with My New Job written in pink glitter bubble letters.

A few months later I frequented sidewalks not intended for baby strollers. Understood that when people claimed I was retro chic, they meant post prime. I'd have to move back to Northern Michigan in order to be beautiful. Each subsequent year was a blunder, like happening upon a pornographic drive-in while hiking through the woods with a junior high boyfriend and his mother.

At least I was the most stable of the pensioners in the vaudeville hotel's lobby bar. A staggering man announced that I hadn't crashed yet. Then he tried to recruit me as a stocking model, and even went so far as to produce a few patented samples. I should not have been so viscerally comforted by the tiny bar of Dial in the bathroom. The towels were cloth towels, disturbingly popular.

One evening my lover was high on something he bought for sixteen dollars in the former bus station turned pigeon sanctuary. We had an argument regarding the definition of *city chicken*. My job was to wear a nylon apron and to walk one straight city block with nobody watching. I was not the one who ended up drinking storm water from a decorative fountain.

When you haven't seen someone for a long time, do not begin the conversation with "I can't believe you're still alive," unless you last saw her shuttled away to the morgue or unsuccessfully defibrillated by a few emergency trainees in a hostel elevator. I have yet to find a jukebox with my favorite song, the one about two identical oxen who enjoyed completely different fates.

DAMAGING MYTHS

I selected the dance that most resembled digging a hole. Nearby we could hear trucks pause, but not stop. I'm not sure what was more unsettling: the costume options for the performance, or the music, which lacked shovels and dirt. It was one hundred percent sky.

All I had was my collection of damaging myths. They fit nicely into a diary, until "first period myths" and later "missed period myths." One bit of advice was to dress a plastic doll up in a red jumpsuit and then purposely lose her in a really obvious place, such as your pants.

Because of my exceptional hearing, I knew the dance instructor had nicknamed me The Outpatient on day one, just like in grad school when a professor jotted *pert* on the roster. It wasn't next to my name. I sat in the corner that was always damp and faced the street.

One holiday gift card was for make your own bandages. The other holiday gift card was for a killer comebacks workshop. Completely redundant. What about run with uneasy foxes, shatter Mama's Waterford crystal, ultimate shoplifting experience?

Before the performance I beat my hair into one terrier-sized extravaganza. It was intractable. Years later, I refused to find my radiographs convincing. I would become the organic apple cider vinegar of my cohort. Everyone would cease believing in my powers.

A RADICAL SUGGESTION

Sometimes we all have too much to drink, and happen to be on a boat. Or in the lobby of a theater, unsure of how to dial out on a payphone. I was accused of being an emotional double agent, a furious hawk, someone worth avoiding, the life of the party, one hell of a life jacket.

Allow me, you said. But there wasn't any further statement. I allowed you. It was like climbing a rope ladder while building a rope ladder. And weaving the rope, and hammering the platform during spare time. If I had kept a journal I would have used the words danger, gravity.

A man spoke to you on the plaza and his name was Lethal Jeff. He liked your sister and he was talking about me. I was so well cared for, my garments maintaining the veneer of their previous owner, who may have been your wife or an undone mannequin called Lethal Sal.

Confession: I purchased a number of blank plaques and awaited their eventual inscription. Vowed to haunt the corner if those inscriptions happened post mortem. Let's creep this lake forever, we decided. Any tree that could live through us might be more than a footnote.

In today's post: *do you think we'll ever go back*? But isn't that the premise of every book? My hospital roommate kept asking when I would cut her hair. Your father owned that hospital, but didn't prepare or serve the awful broths. Unlike you, the hospital forgot to release me.

ELEVATOR PITCH

She wore a wife uniform. Her hands were post-Pine Sol. The entire machinery around her was bedazzled with things not dazzling, such as artificial diamond flecks or imitation cinnamon sticks, the kind that are actually tampons and have to be purchased at a specialty store. She did the math, but only once a month.

Her mother hand-painted an entire replica village, but it was not Victorian. Mid-sixties central Illinois, the biggest conflict in town a battle between grocery chains. The man who would eventually destroy me stood beside a green sedan and breathed a body full of the local factories before driving into soy fields.

However, he was the size of pencil eraser, so his voice was caught by nostalgic awnings and deflected down a toy sewer grate. The wife uniform hovered over this grate for sixteen seasons, hoping to catch something. Meanwhile, I was born on the other side of the continent, already making poor decisions.

Once my aunt let me put dollhouse figures into a pot and turn the burner up. We called this the human condition. I got sneaky in the basement and tried on mildew-tinged wife uniforms (commando) and then settled down with some blank paper and Carole King and a half dozen ghost cigarettes of yesteryear.

In retrospect, the hero was absent for most of his scenes, but that didn't mean he was missing. His corduroy trousers ended up in the cat pan, but that was thanks to the cat, out of uniform and not being editorial in the least. The wife hung her broom up and disappeared, just another bubble in a bucket.

THE WRONG IDEA

Seattle arrived eighteen years too late. I was ready as a damp cage. It took three months to beat what I thought was a chronic case of enthusiasm. Even with a handwritten sign that said *find me*, I remained an ordinary component of the bus station. Perhaps I needed a proper destination.

The next letter began with are you still alive, much like the last. Back then the web was something that snared a lover's wife as she inspected objects under the bed. I was a small bundle of plans. The weather became violent, but we had no way of preparing for it, and survived.

Management said we couldn't bring the forest animals indoors, no matter how cold. They would get the wrong idea. I knew a man who built a wooden throne for his battery powered radio. In those latitudes, a beautiful loser was far more common than a gorgeous stranger.

I paid fifty dollars for a lecture about the dangers of salt. The speaker was self-taught. I realized I would never be able to go back, but I went back, and then I went back again. The survey was not supposed to be double sided, regardless of the earth's preferences.

We never finished recreating all those scenes from our least favorite novels, but I did eventually purchase a rocking chair for my oblivion. I was a map slipped under a stranger's door. Despite all the engineered pitfalls, I remember no instance of being rescued.

THERE'S ONLY ONE STORY

The assistant manager blooms into a manager overnight. I wake hungry, like I've been sleep-running, and there's a calculator under the pillow. Its glow confirms that everyone has forgotten the old math, how it grouped people together and encouraged them to share chairs.

My old building had a level called The Rathskeller. It was for fucking. We knew it was for fucking, but resisted the urge. When approached by strangers in orange vests, our reply was a volley of near-French. Then a few hand gestures that indicated our refusal to comply.

You might imagine the cry of the assistant manager to be like that of a machine rocked off its moorings. Decorate that new office with eucalyptus fronds and the photo of the two of you, back when smoking in the hotel lobby was neither verboten nor uncommon.

I carried my lunch in a paper bag and felt not shameful so much as dishonest, because it was mostly shredded chronicles. Why this is my dream every night, and not a sultry reunion involving pristine non-Midwestern beaches and release time, I do not know.

Learn this sooner than later: everybody is looking for the same person. There's absolutely no fuel for love, so don't pretend to invent one. Somewhere, behind world-weary mini-blinds, the assistant manager takes off a blazer and wonders why it's named after fire.

YOUR SO-CALLED WIFE

There were a couple of those "transcendent moments" such as the scene where we strolled into an event missing several key items and went straight for the dessert cart like jackals. Or when we refused to stop kissing in class, which was gross, but only to everyone else. I brought an entire cassata cake into the office but nobody touched it because they thought we made it.

All of my extant works were on the ease with which we tamed the animals of the new country. Not just feeding, but riding. Sometimes even bathing, which is something you did not attempt frequently enough, unless "falling into a river" counted, but that was more of a country baptism. For two relatively urban adults we sure embraced our shared folk traditions.

In the survey I failed to adequately justify my response to the question: "Could someone ordinary be loved with intensity?" I pondered it the way I told myself if things went wrong enough I'd fall back out. Trade the new jacket for the old one with the zippers. Stand around at twilight. Count things into empty snack food wrappers, and then run.

It's hard to think of yourself as just part of a series. Years previous, I had "a number." This predates the bar code. I would jot it on the ledger, and then a lady would slide the glass open just wide enough for the clipboard. You were experiencing some legal ramifications of unnamed origin. My answer for everything was tuberculosis, but that was a lie.

When the man with the bloody mouth spoke to you of the beauty of your "wife," neither of us corrected him. It was like booking a room in a hotel, then sitting in the lobby all night. Every time I step through the front window of an establishment on a sultry afternoon, I might as well be banishing the law of thresholds. The one that says we're only one person.

OKTOBERFEST SYNDROME

The safe deposit box seemed content enough in its confines. At least it was safe, right? Not an inch of wiggle room on any side. Complete absence of spiders, except the keyhole variety, which usually remained in bundles of ugly dollars that were sent to money jail. A former employee said that money jail was an incinerator, but he also claimed that sometimes counter clerks made their own donuts on the knockoff antique lamps in the "sitting area," and that wasn't true.

There are some disgusting places to store a child's baby teeth after the fiscal exchange under pillows. I really hope you never absently grabbed that decorative stein from yesteryear's Oktoberfest and filled it to the brim with cider, only to take in an accidental mouthful of capsized nibblers. Or romanced a lady and handed her the box that did not contain a quirky brooch from your departed aunt, but rather the remains of an overbite and some mysterious taffeta.

When you said you were up for anything, did that include midnight? Every midnight? After some hustling around the block undetected, gazing into windows where the domesticity was thicker? One a house went up for sale, and it took you weeks to gain courage to take one of the flyers. Apparently it had ".5 bathrooms." Some odd, sinister crops grew in the garden. A bird that looked like a crane huddled in a stand of rhubarb leaves.

I was the type of person who would name a restaurant after a beloved cat, and then cry every day before work. Even if I was one of the "friendly Americans," I did not appear authentic. Felt most comfortable using toy scissors and pretend knives, the kind that would be brandished at a gangland tea party. When asked if there were any old country techniques for weeping eggplant, I pretended not to speak English, which I usually only do on the bus.

Please don't think less of me, but I no longer believe that anyone has a season. Pitch tents, round up the little girls and paint red circles on their cheeks, but I will still recall a simpler time and feel disgusted. Counting dollar bills gets easier, but that leaves you with answers to all the riddles, mystery dead in its worst boots. You get older, and fewer days involve horses, until eventually you can't remember their smell, or how it felt to run away.

HARD DRUGS

We located some drugs but they were soft as a duck's down. One was basically like holding your breath because you aren't expecting to find a river, and then you discover yourself on the listening end of a conversation about bat habits, and then suddenly it's right there eschewing its banks, and you have absolutely no control over whether or not you take off your shoes and leap in, even if there's visible debris flowing (ramen sleeves, shoelaces). You can blame this on your interlocutor or the bats themselves and their instability, or on ancestors who either drowned or made a living by not drowning and managed to retrieve lost items like pocket watches and kids and the dollar bills that your kin so wantonly dispatched to the wind in the opening salvo of their traveling shell game.

I waited six hours on the appointed bench. Long enough for the circus train to unpack its tamer beasts and leave them under my care, because clearly I had been stood up attempting to purchase hard drugs, maybe in exchange for a deep woodland hand job, or just because I was the last person who would be searched at the customs checkpoint, due to the fluency of my cleavage. So there I was, trying to look like I was aspiring to buy some hard drugs and wishing I was another sort of person altogether, the kind who would be happy with stealing a spoon of walnut meats from the ice cream shop and then hosting a sleepover to discuss this transgression with all her closest friends who had never snuck a thing in their lives.

In health class they brought in an officer and a poster board that was supposed to have tiny samples of real drugs, including hard drugs, and I knew better than to volunteer as taste tester, having previously made a gaffe involving resuscitation Annie, who spoke to me a little (flashbacks caused by hard drugs) and said that she wanted to stay dead, so my abstention was conscientious. The officer this year was hot. How challenging it was not to offer him a cold drink and some hard drugs! In the Q&A I asked about the locations of the most insidious party houses in Midland County, but back then we didn't have GPS, so we just had to close our eyes and visualize a blood-spattered stocking hung in the stand of evergreens, a pink neon Swatch phone in the front window.

When I had to lecture a class of elementary school students I was mostly successful in avoiding the topic of relativism. Some of my parables, however, might have been considered "leading" by a court of law, but what did I know of court? These police dramas today have the perp ditching a conspicuous camo L.L. Bean lunch sack full of hard drugs in the town's Little Library, then stopping to selfie with the blue lights behind, when back in the day all we needed was our Chucks, the cry of a distant freight train, and a little hot pee running down our legs. I tell the second graders how most of the hard drugs now are cut with baby aspirin, and they're all like what's aspirin, and then I decide to switch gears and tell a seasonal ghost story called The Haunted Hard Drugs.

The first question is often, "Are the drugs hard to begin with, and if not, how do you get them hard, and do you have to use your hand?" But that's not included in the film strip *Hard Drugs, Death, and You*, which I am asked to watch in the company of other community members with similar interests, and when they get to the part with the poorly calibrated triple beam we're all like "That's fake!" at the same time, in unison, and then the candidates for mayor happen to stroll by the fishbowl we're seated in, since clearly we are a bloc with a united mission and shared vision of the future, and next thing we're getting stiff blue ball point pens and filling out voter registration cards under the names we prefer when dealing and/or purchasing hard drugs, in which case my name is Grace Jones, who I later learn is someone else entirely.

TEMPORARY CROWN

Nobody promised that there would be men in the woods. They didn't have to. Occasionally our walks took us past the acceptable perimeter of town. I always seemed to be wearing something too small those days, or my sweater would get snagged on a stand of juvenile pin oaks, stripping me down to a white camisole. When the men asked me what I wanted to drink, I said *yes, please.*

If I flattened myself against the beefiest tree trunk, I was undetectable. If I didn't breathe too hard, I might have been a breeze. In my last stage performance, each of the girls had a different colored gown, with matching eye shadow, like in old movies where cartoon deer bore certain pastel shades. Maybe it was wrong that my hue was goldenrod, which should be kept far from orifices, and burned in metal bins by the roadside.

Oh, Pauline. Who else would stand outside the JC Penney catalog store in wings? I was barely a teenager when we found a book of blank checks, and abused my mature cursive. Only a few years earlier we had jacked every panel of our blouses with typing paper. My first stop was the shoe store, but only because I was trying to indulge in a stereotype. Later we arrived at dance class with hot sauce on our leotards. I left the waitress a tip of seven dollars and $^{00}/_{100}$ cents.

When our town announced the coming jubilee, my thoughts turned to bears in regalia. This was not a town that consulted its thesaurus. Before the mall went up, everyone waited outside the single-screen, even if the movie was once again *An Animated*

History of the Constitution. Pauline spilled an entire box of Sno-Caps into her lap, and didn't flinch. I began to design my own mascot, but kept the ideas to myself.

The first time you attempt dancing in an outhouse, the quarters may seem unnecessarily dark. It's not the closeness, but the cracks of light, which in another scenario might be termed *organic, neo-primitive.* We've all danced without music, chased by a husky bee during peak season. Somehow the most lethal friend is the one who hitchhikes the best, accepting damp blankets, finding all the top radio stations where every song is the sound of a bedroom fan.

SHARED GOVERNANCE

Somebody had to be the captain. It was one of those days where flowers dispatch their least valuable petals into the wind. A prank caller dialed the number of his own father and demanded more affordable benefits. So would you, if you woke to a door draped with moss.

I named my first sled Central Intelligence. It was plastic, a slight barrier from the elements. Everyone was amazed at how the entire junior high class replicated the dances shown on the film strip, right down to the death knell, which involved props and a harrowing icicle solo.

In the old neighborhood we had to coerce the pipes in winter. Adelaide sang to them. We didn't need to know the language to understand those songs were angry. Thirty years later I would be speaking to a large group about attrition, wearing an electrical tape bracelet.

More than ten survey respondents complained of low moral, not morale, even if one led to the other in certain instances. Marzipan underpants to celebrate a new fiscal year. Subscriptions to counterfeit trade magazines. Dead fish purchased to replace the live ones.

My goal was to become a woman whose clothes smelled like candles. Somebody who could work any sort of coin locker, even the ones with no holes for the coins. An idea is both a box and its contents, said my favorite philosopher. Or perhaps that was me.

THE BLUE NOTE

Once we built a toy guillotine and instantly felt terrible about it. I erased the cross messages I had written on the dry erase board, a double dark note regarding fish sticks in the microwave. Have you ever stood on an ornamental deck and viewed sixteen raccoons filing into the attic next door? Did you offer them a section of your orange? One day you will be one of those raccoons, peeling away aluminum siding to reveal hundreds of square feet of the unknown.

Sometimes you listen to a jazz band in a dress that appeared in the back seat of your Corolla. You shrug it on right there in the parking deck, risking exposure and feeling immediately intoxicated. In medieval literature this dress would be a poison mantle braided over decades by your most passionate enemy. But nobody cares enough to hate you. Even the postal workers congregate on your front porch, which is more a pie stand than a speakeasy.

I'm still waiting to receive my "I almost died on public transport" t-shirt. Silly how someone can mistake an anesthesiologist for a god. Remember how the third rail looked better when doubled-over? Nobody tried to help, presumed I was some new kind of hustler. The bus never came so I pounded on an empty car window before walking. Eventually they pitched morphine into my arm in front of three kids who peeked under the curtain like story hour.

Have you heard the ditty called Oh Buttermilk Pie? Have you tasted the awful cascades of an unpracticed saxophone player? Listen: I got here. The magazine article I pretend to read in the waiting room reminds me that many people haven't. My friend disappeared from earth four years ago, when I was just a phone passed around during Katrina, some roommate obsessing over lost yearbooks. The cat was safe. I went forward into my business.

FAVORITE HAINTS

After the U-Haul broke down and you were doused with hot oil on the side of the highway, I walked to the nearest exit and there was a turquoise motel that matched my jacket. Since it was the desert I did not need a jacket. It wasn't really the desert. It was Kansas, the part that is completely empty. And maybe calling that garment a jacket is being too generous. It was a terrycloth tube top, only with straps and an oversized, non-functioning bow in the back, which at a distance made me look like a piece of wind-up machinery, perhaps a Christmas mouse awaiting her brother at a foggy window, and when he arrived with the eggs or the holiday goose he'd blown a guy for as a trade, she would clap her mechanical hands and spin around until somebody snapped a tiny switch.

The cashier at the motel kept asking me about my favorite haints. The poor thing didn't know what she was getting into, and I believe her Chihuahua grew aged and anemic halfway through my account, which included gestures that were fueled by the Tab she offered me, and the generous nature of an avocado vinyl chair where my bones fit perfectly like I, too, was created in 1965 as part of a mass market venture bringing the present day's style to corners of the country that usually relied upon old staples such as the folding chair or prefabricated porch lounger. After an hour or two, I had to excuse myself to use the facilities, and truth be told, I washed my armpits because ghost stories make me rowdy and that motel stocked a soap that pounded its guests with instant nostalgia: pink as bubble gum, haunted by witch hazel.

Before I left, the cashier asked me to help untangle a bird from some fishing line. Though I found this implausible out there in the desert where the only water was the toilet or the humping in the ice machine, I wasn't in a place to ask questions. The bird was actually somebody's finger, and not even the middle finger, so I shared the story about how that truck engine erupted as if somebody without a license in tinkering had tinkered. I believe the Chihuahua demonstrated signs of empathy. It wasn't the first time I had traveled to a place unsuccessfully and left with a large quantity of decades-old *National Geographic*s. Not a soul in the motel had heard the tale of the vanishing anchor, and so I showed them my tattoo as some indisputable proof.

THE BIG TIME

That summer we were all big timing. Even while subsisting on
diet grape soda and cup o' noodles and red dots of
pseudoephedrine. We decided to become the *Let me on this bus with
my dog* type. We boarded the train at a pretentious street, like
someone would mistake us for rich. I had a temporary job at a
comedy club nicknamed Fecund City.

I would never make money as a dancer. We tried to escape town
in an '87 Sunbird. Even the carnival ended up being a let-
down once we realized they rolled out the burning cinnamon
dough and neon every damn night. Our carnival had a number
of improvised rides like "The Squirmatron," which was
unsanctioned. I preferred a stiff run through cornstalks.

I wouldn't give a man a cigarette and he accused me of Lady Di-
ing and waved the finger. I buried my college brochures double
deep in the experimental corn plot, but they ended up back in
our mailbox, along with some mysterious intervention
planning paperwork intended for another address. I have
never believed in coincidences.

People surround themselves with abominations such as
artificial cheese and real leather. I would big time a parking
attendant if it would improve my perspective. I might big time
myself, my next of kin, or perhaps even my favorite stranger. I
know it's gross, but I would love to be tall enough to rip things
apart and blame it on nature.

ZERO TOLERANCE POLICY

Thirty minutes after accidentally signing off on a letter with "up yours" instead of "your devoted servant," the numbness came back. Fringed edges of my recent holding pattern rippled in the wind. I drove directly to the store for Cheetos, had a panic attack before cutting the ignition. But then I gathered up the courage. I always gathered up the courage, except when I did not.

How much touching is enough? If you have to ask that question, you are likely in violation. However, past work as an unlicensed hair braider makes thresholds subjective. Past work in risk management made me never again ask about AD&D, which is not an ointment. There are places you should not return to, and the same goes for bodies that used to be yours but stopped.

Let's say this is a win back story. Pick your poison, the bartender said, but he was no winner. I can't help believing that my younger years were so much classier. You could smoke in the lobby bar of the Palmer House. I had dresses small enough to stuff into a miniature vanity purse. I could fall face first into a carpet and appreciate the luxury of baroque swirls.

I was the kind of person who put a photograph of her naked back on the cover of her debut chapbook. Clearly that was before my front advanced to major asset. Thirty minutes after committing to a minor role in a win back story, I considered changing my phone number. The scout had a clipboard like all scouts. There was a bit of pinching but that was expected.

Asked how I financed my education, I describe the great swaths of shoddily-scanned text corrected, the supple transcription peddle (closest thing I had to a car then), raw articles of incorporation brandished hot out of the mimeograph's mouth. These days, I have no sort of tolerance whatsoever, just a constellation of outdated bullet points, some ancient train noise.

PARTIAL GENIUS

Being a cigarette girl was nothing like being a suicide girl but whatever. Try explaining to an eclectic readership that your only comfort is the sound of rain against a dormer window. Once I had a cold reading in a rehabilitation home basement. It reminded me of a shooting gallery with all that nodding and nobody particularly alarmed. Also the covert counting of small bills. You had to ask a lady to watch the door to the bathroom, and if you took more than ten minutes somebody started pounding. I was only able to offer customers two choices: kings or ultra-lights.

Things I could not get clean enough for you: politics, cuffs of trousers, the entire fleet of public transportation, air and water, tropes of fine literature, religion (but not mythology— that was okay), croutons lost in their shaggy wonderland, my past, the final page of your checking account register, peals of Bob Seger even though we were in an actual church rather than "the church of erotic ecstasy," the sirens that you used as an excuse for walking faster, anything not related to the body because it wasn't supposed to be clean, and allcluia at least I did that right.

I held the hand-sized radio in my palm and wished it could be implanted in my chest. Not instead of a heart. As a sort of companion to a heart. It could only play one song, however, or else it would bleed out. That's a heavy commitment, presuming life has multiple decades. Multiple favorite sweaters dropped to the floor of someone's living room. That's a lot of living if it's actually lived. Rolling down the stairs like spilled marbles. Exhumed from a backyard like a thimble that slipped away. Some Motown hit poorly remade several decades later.

We decided to name a certain hour *the melancholy hour*, but then fought over when it would be (morning was both sad and triumphant, there was most likely thunder at twilight, dinnertime was packed with morose wives and their dreams of increased square footage, middle of the night was only for trips to the loo). In retrospect, most of my memories are about novels. Did I even own a wing chair, or just the impression of one upon my back? Was that us, or a story about two characters with similar motivations? The novels never answered.

Confession: I was only a partial genius. Please don't say it was the parts you left in me, because that wasn't much. In between checking the knobs on my gas stove, I worried about immortality. We should have been the subject of at least one plaque by now, one tribute panel at a major literary conference. My first time at the major literary conference we just huddled on a couch touching each other's badges. Then we got lost in our own city, like a couple of housecats. At least my genius was a little bit flashy and held market value. You were a wallet filled with questionable credit.

A LITTLE NIGHT SKY

I was like a person tied to the train tracks, only I secured the ropes myself and was just planning to swallow a little night sky when everything aligned. Your friend Charlie was making a film and I had to hold the black umbrella and wear a dress with snaps up the front. Kids chased an albino squirrel as if this was a work of domestic realism about an assassin and her sexy assistant who decide to give it all up for a musty Victorian in the seat of Wood County, but then instead they create a whole lot more people and those people are small and don't know how to shut the fuck up.

You look like the addicted to love video isn't what you meant to say, and I forgive you, but it has taken me a while. It was a decade of rough transitions and sometimes I resented when you said I hung posters wrong or were annoyed at how much I liked broth, which to you was just an idea. I had a leather jacket I wished was yours but it wasn't and that's probably for the best because one of us lost it and neither remembers. Back then there was no such thing as a portable camera, only Charlie with his boom and the amateurish sketches I made of you and then hid in books at the library.

It wasn't because we left my jacket. All the apartments were identical and echoed similarly, yielded when pushed by various hands, required similar minutes for hot water to materialize. In the dream a mailbox held just a few letters of my last name clinging to metal. Everything slow as a dial-up connection. Library elevator a cage with a few cracked buttons. That dripping sound, birds too stupid to know how free they were, all the study chairs pulled out and pushed in like a fin de siècle machine shop or the shooting gallery we walked into accidentally and then stayed and then went back.

What do you do with knowledge of someone's least favorite desserts and preferred fabrics when they have hitched the proverbial wagon and moved west? I stood blinking in disbelief at the ice storm. I stood blinking in disbelief at my own disbelief. Nobody counted my eyelashes or turned the burners down so low they looked like ghost eyes. I started storing jewelry in my largest pots. Knocked on door after door. Dialed parts of phone numbers. Went to a festival alone with a purse that looked like a tackle box, drank ugly whiskey. Deliberated unkindly with myself and others.

Let's say there was a map but you didn't own it and neither did I. Somebody zipped that jacket around a tree. Maybe after that they broke glass and ate day-old bear claws. That's a donut, I said. In our worst fight we deployed all of our respective intellectual jargon in opposite directions for absolutely no purpose. "*Interdisciplinary* is an inappropriate word for pillow talk but that's only because it's so common in academia" was your rationale. My rationale was like the awful craft thing I made with yarn in sixth grade and I cheered because it was finished, even if mostly knots.

SAINT GERMAIN DES PRÉS

Imagine being burned down and then rebuilt only slightly different. Is it too late? Perhaps. There may be permits and other obstacles to consider. Acute lack of a notary public. It's always best to rely on your sanity in legal situations. Except this one.

Pretend you have never languished on a wooden deck a hundred or so feet above a dead lawn. Grolsch and the opiate noise of Rod Stewart. Did your outfit really consist of assorted bandanas? Was the best part of that afternoon the shaking?

It takes about thirty minutes in the waiting room before you realize every pamphlet has the same woman on its front panel. Crack cocaine addiction and cervical dysplasia and anorexia nervosa. The carpet is different in each examination room, however.

Nobody's asking you to "speak openly about your travails," and if they are, they probably want to see your passport. In oils class you were once commanded to paint your way out of a nightmare. The customs agent isn't asking for similar.

If you're on the floor and it's dark, a disco ball will be the most resplendent lover. Steal a ladder and pull one down and smuggle it into the restroom to consult your reflection. You will see the brackets of your future a hundred times over.

Certain people live the mantra: someday I will get back to Paris. Eventually it becomes a metaphor. Instead try: someday I will be the best doorstop possible. Someday I'll hold the prettiest pins, neighbor to the jolliest rickrack under our sun.

HISTORY TOWN

First the teenagers rebelled against history, and then they internalized it. Modern sex, modern sex, historical sex and decades thereof. So what if nobody bathed. Who cared if a little lace got snagged in the charger cable. The teenagers sought the most cutting-edge snacks fathomable: those cakes made with dry ice, sandwiches that illuminated the customer's stomach hours later. Then, the reverse, and the homecoming queen was fighting the French club president over an exhumed cast iron skillet and some eggs that may have fallen from a hen or something more primitive.

So how to rationalize what we called "the reenactments," which were either a barn-raising or building a phone that fit in one nostril and played music with subtle vibrations. Half the senior class wanted throbbing EDM, the remainder voting for a sole, blindfolded fiddle player in the corner. When the bell rang everyone ran out the door to their respective butter churns and lasers and to catch crawdads with either some old pantyhose or a replica of the Edmund Fitzgerald or bare hands, which readily walked in both worlds at once, though more historically acceptable if gloved.

When your town's main industry is the history, it's easy to regress, though nobody was pleased when dresses had to be imported from the neighboring town's dead lady closets, old-timey post cards forged, all cameo brooches snatched up from the case as soon as a store owner pricked them into velvet. Never ask, "How long can antiquing be considered a sustainable practice?" After all, they recycled. Buried coffee grounds and hoped an old-fashioned bicycle would grow amidst the heirloom squash, ready to net a handsome price from some suburban fudge-seekers.

And what about when those teenagers went to university, beyond the vocational offerings of History Town Community College, where Joshua kept asking why you could not breed a peacock with a goat, and the mayor's daughter dressed in full robot before stiff-legging into Communications 101 with zero books in her backpack. And what about early-onset puberty? Middle-schoolers already in full historic dress, wondering what year pendulums had been invented, and whether theirs would swing back like that famous futuristic movie where the hero melts into a thread of steel.

SOMETHING HARD

They commended our ease, but actually things were really hard. Standing like that? Pretending looks didn't matter? Pretending looks mattered? It was like putting together a piece of furniture that was never intended to stand. And our lives depended on it. Despite being boring and stupid. We slipped into pants, and then we took them off, and often it was for no reason.

Little did we know: it would not get better, even when the pants got bigger and the furniture proportions involved slightly less particleboard, more actual wood. Several coffee cups to choose from, on different shelves, but nothing ever seeming full. We became owners of mattresses, and the mattresses just planked there mockingly as we buttoned trousers and ignored the mirror.

The younger versions of ourselves only thought of where the train was going, not considering the sparks made by the rails, wondering what crouched in the tall grasses blanketing stops long abandoned. A roof was smoking, and it made us think about a summer barbecue, washing the cars with that floppy sponge the size of a brick, tying and untying our halter top straps.

It didn't exactly make us proud that we had vomited in the restroom of every diner downtown, but we didn't lie in bed shuddering about it like we do now, reliving humiliating small talk, recalling slights made accidentally at the Woolworth's soda counter in 1987, honking a horn and watching a cyclist fall into a prickly bush, dropping her glass milk bottle.

When we fell on our asses on the dance floor on a night we weren't getting paid, it was nothing to pop right back up like it was yet another move. And now we think, maybe we will just use a heel to grind this pencil into the sidewalk until it's gone, instead of picking it up. Perhaps we will not get off the train. There are worse places to settle in and wait.

UNTAMED THICKETS

I loved being tagged as other people's wives, sometimes by other people's wives, and by tagged I mean swatted, not tagged on the internet or with sensuous roils of Old English graffiti. When the celebrity asked me to sign his record was it vinyl or legal? I always had twelve pens or none. My cupboards either bursting with all the essentials needed to survive an apocalyptic Midwestern winter, or spare like I was living in IKEA, with hardly a noodle to eat in a flood.

I matriculated into a degree granting program on punishments. This followed my Associates in Discipline Studies, which went by as slowly as ants contemplating ennui. All my favorite sandwich shops closed up shop, and due to intoxication and intermittent nausea I just couldn't fathom it. What about that one night with the faux Reuben, the waitress wearing a cherry-patterned apron as she refilled my avalanche of home-chipped chips? What could be more enduring?

My new apartment had carpet on the walls. I wasn't sure what to think but felt a little more free playing my 90s techno mixes at odd hours. Years ago I used to hand-trim rugs the way some hand-trim their rugs. My mixtape covers were not duplicated, they were engineered. I thought about throwing it all away and working with stone, but then recalled my privilege. Everyone was trying their best to regress: paleo on the table, tending dangerous pets, sex in untamed thickets.

I did a lot of really dumb things, like jumping out of cars and allowing my feelings to seep into the pad under the carpet. Interrupted conversations in the diner to speak about my magic, using my full name like that would make a difference. Certain nights were so hot I just loomed on stairways waiting for someone to push me aside, which isn't a punishment like making out with a man who hurt you, in a closet filled with electrified metal hangers, and then missing it.

SEXY FUGITIVE COSTUME

The woman has been located and is unharmed, was simply riding the bus all night with a few bags of plastic beads that appeared to be something more sinister, though nobody knows what exactly. Every search party member should tuck away his or her erection and start wondering what's on TV, other than coverage of how the woman has been located, maybe even a primitive reenactment with a mannequin and a fringed denim handbag and what looks like a deflated cootie catcher from sixth grade where every fortune reads "hot stuff."

All neighborhood watches (neighborhoods watch? neighborhood watchers? watchers who stand behind damp towels in the kitchen windows of neighborhoods?) should go back to justifying the value of mushrooms in a traditional steakhouse, the type where ladies start hiking their skirts on the way to the powder room. The aldermen should roll up the tinted windows of their aldermanic Navigators, some cartoon playing not for kids but to make the speed work double duty, easier to talk fast in the presence of a hot pink clown with ragged stitches.

It's embarrassing when your friend's mom calls your mom and then stops by and smokes a cigarette in your extremely pristine dining room because your friend is missing and there's a treacherous bridge involved, or so the first witness proclaims from the luxurious confines of her *Make Mine a Double* tank top. In the background, some kids lower their knee-length shorts and display a loaf's worth of ass crack to the cameras. Somewhere in the dark, a stranger is loving his own reflection in the bakery window, the klieg lights providing just the right angle.

"If people want to be touched so badly, why don't they just get married?" was the comedian's most famous punchline, and the woman watched it in closed captioning at the check cashing place while trying out some new signatures. It was one of those nights that either warranted a fresh tattoo or a trip to the craft store. Hours later, we see her blazing into the back of a police car but just, as the reporter says, as a precaution because so many people are looking for her, and it's a good thing nobody drinks dairy milk anymore because she'd be on every carton.

You get older, and suddenly it's no longer practice. If you dress up like a fugitive, maybe you are one. The same goes for a Raggedy Ann pirate, a squirrel with nut-packed cheeks. The woman hopes it's a different bus driver this time, the one who treats her like a clueless tourist rather than an escapee from the halfway house uptown. All concerned citizens should dip their respective backsides into a deep recliner or a tepid bath. Stow the flashlights. Discard all lines composed to be spoken into a news microphone: *She clung to me like a live deer in a dead lake.*

SONG OF THE FRENCH CLUB PRESIDENT

I was preoccupied with my annual migration. It was almost as troublesome as a sidewalk sale, but with fewer swampy-eyed pedestrians. To think that over twenty years ago I had been the French club president, who refused to speak to anyone in English, flung inauthentic pastries into the nearest trash compactor. My sandals sounded like gunshots and I loved it.

At graduation, my parting message began with "this school has no Jesus," and it didn't. Months later I would be packed into a college auditorium with all the other former French club presidents from the tri-state area. The ones who had never actually been to France were asked to sit behind pillars or out in the lobby. Or at least that's what I think happened, because the directions did not apply to me.

The best of us brought a sack filled with back issues of *Marie Claire*, a Jean-Jacques Goldman album or several. In terms of fashion, we could wear anything: scarves in the pool, thong leotards in geometry class, fragrance so profound it wouldn't leave the sinuses for decades. Maybe it's still here, in my dim Renault, companion on every migration with each seeming the last.

Even in modern day situations, former French club presidents listen to all the music people fucked to in the early 90s. Except the power ballads, which remind too strongly of farewells to our favorite exchange students, the ones whose cool we would ride into the millennium. When strangers shout in my face "where are you from?" it's one Esprit smack away from an obvious answer.

Where do all the former club presidents go when divorced and suffering? Bake sales of yesteryear burned along with the parts of the brain that erase first with the coke. Café au lait, faux Madeleines. *Crème fraiche* might be a pretentious name for a Yorkie, but a great icebreaker when seated across from your suburban counterpart, day planner rolling with continental script.

GIVING UP THE GHOST

If you are afraid of history then avoid tinctures. Disobey traditional recipes. Incinerate evidence including recent receipts and the ribbons that flowed from your hair as recently as 2001. Pray for mild derailments of trains that shuttled you safely to the jobs where you remain best loved ghost. Most likely to return to the vending machine. Frequenter of the hot cocoa packets even in early August. The only creature seen reading Russian novels during the fifteen minute lunch and then sleeping beneath oak trees on the property after work.

When I say I am part cat, I also mean every animal that has ever walked through me, which is a number too large to discuss. Often I start and remember I'm here, and it's now, like a fugue state patient in a crime drama except my hair is probably longer and the panic is invented. In high school everyone loved and feared "the fishbowl" but in reality we were each more invisible than the last version of us, now either watching our children multiply or standing at the same corner with a slightly slimmer cigarette and new swears.

It's hard to remember back before I learned to drive but it's not like things went any slower. It's just one of many false markers. How many days since you began your last panic, since the beginning of your latest obsession, since you figured how best to calibrate the eyelash adhesive? The ghost told me shoplifting was right and made me follow the wrong girls into the fitting room. I wore trash t-shirts and cutoffs with unknown flags painted on them, legs like how our fields looked after a particularly devastating summer of drought agriculture.

The guy was on tether but that didn't stop me from kissing him pretty hard at the antique warehouse where he worked under police supervision. So many variations on Santa that some were basically a thumb of silly putty with two cloves and a little Vaseline and what looked like blood. Gummy candy with a wet center. Gloves owned by the lady alleged of murder as recently as 1897, kept in a case under lockdown per order of the authorities. A devastating collection of post cards home that were either never delivered or discarded, or sent back into the war they came from.

LOVE SONGS OF 1992

Eventually you lose the need to carry three plates at once. Then you lose the ability to carry three plates at once. But that will not stop you from trying, like when you make seven attempts at remembering your PIN after four glasses of wine and a modest serving of shrimp cocktail. When the waiter carries it out, you think of a hand perched in a pewter champagne glass. When swearing at the ATM, your fingers are an actionable oxymoron.

Love songs of 1992 no longer work. Their kind of love is obsolete, like an outdated version of PeopleSoft that assigns each employee a primary color and nothing further. Imagine if you were determined a lackluster medium blue, listening to The Sundays while recalling a recipe from decades ago, the one you got fired over when you copied trade secrets. Since there was no internet, you had to write the details on people's hands at the mall.

I asked for *Dead Malls of America* but got *Dead America* in my stocking instead. I was too much of an introvert to petition for help at the Estée Lauder counter. It would be like begging my grandmother to help me latch some garters. In my neighborhood we had a Block Mother. In panic dreams I still show up at her doorstep with a mouth full of blood dressed in half my pajamas. That house is now up for sale: $15K and offered as-is.

At CVS I think about asking a guy in a bowtie why anyone would wear a bowtie in CVS, but lose my nerve when the radio switches to the Love Songs of 1992 channel. Does it count as a party if you're the only one dancing? I'm just looking for a basket, that's the name of the dance, and it's intense. I wish I had old recordings of myself just talking, because in retrospect it seems like my head in 1992 was filled with orange juice and gaps.

Some day you'll be hate-watching a Netflix series about your generation, and the "you" of the series will be disappointing: caring too much about her poetry, making the cosmetician wipe off all the eyeliner and do it over with electric blue. She'll have one boyfriend in season one. Watch as she balances six plates with her meager wingspan, like the cartoon about your generation that inspired such a music revival that everyone fell in or out of love.

FREE AGENCY

When everything in a life is conventional, it's difficult to avoid digging a hole. I started on my way home from school, thinking a quick rest for the next day. Proximity to bulbs told me beauty was possible. My bones were sturdier than remnants of a possum. I rose like something conjured.

The first time I slept outdoors I used a map as a blanket. Warmed my feet with the serene ears of a wild dog. Deepened the hole. Stepped back to consider its dimensions. Pushed away thoughts of revenge. All the birds in my field guide were long asleep, and were safer that way.

Eventually wanderings lost their charm. I mean that literally. The roads were ordinary. Perhaps it was an ill combination: full meal including bread and soup, half hour staring into a fire, superficial talk of books. I should have starved and put my clothes on wet. Invited the night under my skirt.

If asked what my favorite color was, I said clear. It was the closest truth I could find. Decades ago, somebody buried string along the perimeter of the yard, but it felt like electrified wire, or I felt like electrified wire, before wire was invented, back when electricity was just a witch tale.

As our roof collapsed, I prayed fire would take the antique photo album, leave the metal drinking glass that made milk taste like blood. I spent a few hours in the town square, contemplating grievances like assorted candies. A past can be burned away, even with simple friction.

FANTASY SPORTS

Painting the faces on baby dolls may sound like a dream job but consider the dream. One twitch and an eye becomes an untoward lane. Show up mad and you'll have the imprint of doll nostrils on your fingertips all night. Imagine the horror of your spouse, the delight of your lover, your own uncertainty pulling a contact lens out at a stoplight and detecting faint powder on the breeze.

True story: eels and humans used to be friends. So when they had to carry me out of the Belle Isle aquarium I was not causing a disturbance but rather exercising compassion for an ancient compatriot. I wanted to be so long and so thin and just as furiously countenanced. Was already living in a murky box with limited light, hideous fake plants, constant taps of fingers.

I signed up for a class on surrogacy but it was not about migrating butterflies so I quit. The guidance counselor identified quitting as my main strength and weakness. Crack cocaine, AP physics, checking and rechecking gas stove knobs before leaving the house, sex with strangers, nail biting, drunk appearances at the animal shelter resulting in near adoptions, transcendental meditation.

Most of the guys who got the *Varsity* tattoo on their birthday now spend evenings drinking Miller Lite next to a bathtub full of the week's dirty dishes. I would remember how they posed on social media except it wasn't invented, and we just had to gossip and draw crude renderings of how things went down. Sometimes we sketched them with sticks in the dirt.

When did desire become just another dangler on a charm bracelet, next to the flamingo or the handcuffs? My friends crushing so hard on Anna Karenina. All I wanted was to play with her hair. And then the decade turned and we started getting off imagining stacks of cash, extra thick credit cards. *Fine, I'll never say anything funny again*, I said, and everyone laughed.

ACKNOWLEDGMENTS

Sincere thanks to the following journals where the following poems first appeared, sometimes in a slightly different form.

Ampersand Review: The Jolly Anchor

Border Crossing: Trouble Shirt

Court Green: Untamed Thickets

Diode: Skill Games

Five Points: Partial Credit Syndrome

Gargoyle: Consolation Prize and Horizon-Free Living

Grimoire: The Craft

The Laurel Review: Notre Dame de Paris, Sacré-Cœur, and Some Truths

Queen of Cups: Voir Dire

Smoking Glue Gun: Sexy Fugitive Costume

Tinderbox Poetry Journal: The Haunted Minute

Waxwing: Fantasy Sports and History Town

Grateful acknowledgment is made to the Ohio Arts Council for their support through an Individual Excellence Award in 2018.

Abundant gratitude to the friends and colleagues who offered their support, including Erica Bernheim, Heather Braun, Oliver de la Paz, Heather Derr-Smith, Chris Drabick, Sarah Dravec, David Giffels, Susan Grimm, Matthew Guenette, Noor Hindi, Thea Ledendecker, Erika Meitner, Jennifer Militello, Jon Miller, Caryl Pagel, Jay Robinson, Austin Seip, Tom Simpson, Amy Bracken Sparks, Elizabeth Tussey, Eric Wasserman, and Alejandra Zanetta.

Special thanks to Julie Brooks Barbour, and to Amy Freels.

Much gratitude to Black Lawrence Press, especially Diane Goettel.

Much love to Eric, Gabi, and Ray, and to my parents.

Mary Biddinger is the author of five previous full-length poetry collections, including *Small Enterprise* and *The Czar*. She teaches literature and creative writing at the University of Akron and NEOMFA program, and edits the Akron Series in Poetry for the University of Akron Press. Poems have recently appeared in *Court Green*, *Poetry*, *Tupelo Quarterly*, and *Waxwing*, among others. Biddinger has been the recipient of three Individual Excellence Awards in poetry from the Ohio Arts Council, a National Endowment for the Arts poetry fellowship, and the 2019 mid-career Cleveland Arts Prize in literature. She is currently at work on a new collection of prose poems, and a manuscript of small poems about ordinary things.